Thrive

A to B Guide to

Motivation

Brian Guest

ISBN No. 978-1-908964-01-4

Thrive

Thrive Careers Ltd.

www.thrive-careers.com

ABOUT THRIVE

Thrive Careers specializes in providing leading career development information, mentoring and coaching products and services to professionals and corporate clients around the world.

Created to support managers and executives with their career challenges and development objectives, Thrive is at its core a promoter of self-development and effective leadership.

This guidebook series, along with Thrive's other product ranges, are designed to suit the objectives and busy schedules of modern day professionals by providing cost-effective expertise, interactivity and flexibility to clients. For more information on our other guidebooks, self-assessment tools, coaching and mentoring products visit our website:

www.thrive-careers.com

Thrive Careers Ltd. is based in London, United Kingdom.

THRIVE A TO B GUIDEBOOKS

This series is written for managers and executives who wish to develop their core skills and those of their teams.

Each guidebook draws on the practical experience of a top executive coach and senior business leader. This breadth of experience helps you see the bigger picture and provides state-of-the-art thinking and tools for achieving positive and sustainable change.

In this series Thrive aims to support and challenge you in your learning and development with a blend of coaching and mentoring approaches. Not only does this grant you access to top quality resources derived from in-depth experience, but also frames them in a way that you can relate to your own circumstances and challenges.

Executive coaching is one of the most powerful and effective ways for leaders and managers to develop their skills and performance. But working one-to-one with a top coach is not always feasible.

The A to B guides give you access to several of the advantages of coaching in a cost-effective and just-in-time approach. You will be constantly challenged to assess your own situation – where you want to get to and how best to get there. It's all about achieving results effectively, efficiently, economically and sustainably. To do this you will be using tools that top professional coaches use with their clients to help you coach yourself and others. You will also be challenged to find the changes that are going to give you the biggest improvement and given advice on how to tackle diverse situations you may encounter.

The series is designed to be easy to work through and to store most of your key notes and plans so that they become working documents. This aspect, coupled with the common structure and layout, make them easy to refer back to and to sustain your learning and progress.

CONTENTS

GETTING THE MOST OUT OF THIS RESOURCE

- Think about yourself, your team and work environment and write down your major motivational challenges. This will help give context and priorities to the development of your motivation and that of your team.

Your top challenges:

_____

_____

_____

_____

Your team's top challenges:

_____

_____

_____

_____

- Review the overall structure first.

- Go through the guidebook in sequence, completing the exercises and self-assessments as set out.

- Get feedback from others as suggested.

- Mark areas you wish to return to think about or understand more fully.

- Highlight areas you believe could be key to your own progress and that resonate strongly with you.

- Follow the guide to producing your own developmental goals using the Challenge-Priority Brainstorming Chart and Thrive Action Plan located in the appendix of this guidebook. Be positive and get going!

- Create a mentor or thinking partner relationship at work to challenge and support you on your journey; someone who you believe has and deserves a good reputation in the area of your developmental need.

- Consider creating a small focus group to meet periodically and share thoughts on particular challenges and dilemmas any of you are facing in this area of development.

- Incorporate a reread of the guide into your action plan.

The A to B Methodology

The A to B methodology is based upon the premise that we have the ability to change and develop in the ways that we really want to.

There are four key questions:

- Where am I? This is "**A**." This sometimes has an element of being "stuck" about it – think of it as a red stoplight impeding you from continuing your journey.

- Where do I need to get to? This is "**B**." Imagine it as the blue sky you see when you reach the top of a mountain that makes you realize just how much you've achieved throughout your journey.

- What barriers are in my way and how can I overcome them?

- What else do I need "**TO**" get there? Think of this as the green traffic light that has come on to let you progress with your journey.

Where you are is where you are. **A** is **A**. It helps to accept this gracefully. Some things have gone well and perhaps some things could have gone better. We can calmly learn from the past, but we cannot let it keep absorbing us, especially if the emotions it evokes are negative for us. Some unwanted or disliked things might seem present in **A**, they may seem to be out of our control. How we react to them inside ourselves, however, is ultimately under our control.

Imagine holding where you are, represented by a big letter **A**, in the open relaxed palm of your left hand (or right hand if you are left-handed), and where you are going, represented by a big letter **B**, in your other palm, which is raised up a foot higher than the other palm. You need to let go of any strong emotions about **A** and feel excited and positive about improving to **B**.

You have particular strengths and development needs. These can depend on circumstances, both inside yourself – for example, your mood, stress or energy levels – or in your external environment – for example, the pressures in your particular business.

Sometimes we can accurately understand our actual position. Sometimes we need input or feedback from others to see our position more clearly. This often applies to motivating others.

We learn best by leveraging our strengths – our learning preferences and building on our positive experiences and talents. Very often we see the glass as half-empty instead of half-full. A positive attitude is important in making progress.

Next you need to know where you want to get to. This needs to be a better place; better in terms of what you value. It might not be perfect, but it is better and will meet most of your priority needs.

Finally, you need a clear plan for what you need to do to get to that better place. You need to identify the challenges and support or resources you need to grow and develop into the new position.

1. INTRODUCTION TO MOTIVATION

Central to achieving personal and corporate goals is the issue of how we motivate ourselves and others.

Motivation can come naturally but sometimes things happen that can cause us to lose motivation just as easily. Just watch a two-year-old child – they can be naturally motivated to try things and to learn. Equally, things they experience as painful can discourage them.

What motivates one person may not motivate another. This is a source of many mistakes – it's easy to assume that what motivates us will motivate others, especially if we feel passionate about something.

This guidebook will help you find the levers and make the improvements you need to motivate yourself and others.

1.1   The four motivations

What motivates you to do what it is that you do?

Are you motivated to avoid pain or to pursue inner satisfaction and pleasure? Answering this question using "the four motivations" (Percy, 1997) – political, economic, emotional and natural internal – is one of the ways of looking at what drives us to do what we do.

1.2   Political motivation

Often we do something because we are compelled by external forces. Fear can prompt this – we can be afraid of the consequences if we do not take action. If this goes on for too long, we can begin to strongly resent the person, group or situation that is frightening us.

Politically-motivated behavior that distances our internal values from our actions can sometimes cause high levels of stress, cynicism, resentment and poor, unsustainable performance.

Example: We may follow the instructions of our boss even though we believe they are wrong or unethical because we are afraid of the consequences of expressing our concerns.

1.3   Economic motivation

Being motivated from an economic perspective will depend on the result of our cost-benefit analysis to the action in question. We act if we can see that the benefits outweigh the costs or if acting gives us the best economic return.

Example: We may not break the speed limit driving a car as we may wish to avoid the fine rather than being motivated by driving in a way that respects the safety of others.

Political and economic motivations are at times strongly influenced by fear and "should" thinking. We are motivated to avoid pain or potential loss. Such behaviors can be less sustainable because they go against our truer underlying values or beliefs.

1.4   Emotional motivation

Here we do what we do because we find joy and emotional satisfaction from the activity – it is pleasurable for us.

Example: We care for the environment because it gives us a sense of joy to experience the nature and to leave the environment in a better state than we found it so others can enjoy it too.

1.5   Deeper motivation

Here we do what we do because we cannot not do it! It flows from some-where deep within us. This often follows some kind of transformational experience that leads us to feel committed to a cause.

Example: An entrepreneur traveling through a tropical rainforest is moved by the plight of the indigenous peoples caused by deforestation. He decides to dedicate his time and energy to founding a company that will introduce a new technology that helps governments and consumers to control illegal trade in timber and to support ethical and sustainable timber businesses.

Motivations founded on our inner beliefs, values and joys are more sus-tainable because they make us feel purposeful and deeply satisfied.

1.6   Combinations of the four motivations

In practice our motivations are rarely pure and we experience elements of all the four motivations. This is part of being human. Along our journey of pursuing a transformational inner motivation there are likely to be times we will be influenced by the other three types of motivation. However, we need to derive most of our inspiration from the emotional and deep inner motivations if our efforts are to be sustainable.

Fear can get a lot of bad press. In excess, or when present at the wrong time, it can be a barrier to success. However, there are times and situations in which, with the right balance with the other positive motivations, fear-based motivations have their place. A slight degree of fear is often mixed with a sense of respect, for example, in our attitude towards a senior executive or boss. We can fear that we will let these people down as we respect them and their position of authority.

Fear is understood to have been driven by the survival instinct – it can have a positive influence in selective situations. Excessive fear can be harmful to long-term performance and no fear whatsoever may not optimize us to perform at our best. So balance and judgment can play a part. Performance nerves can be very positive if we control them well – live performers such as musicians, actors and athletes know that the right dose of performance nerves can help them achieve their best.

Our motivations can change over time too. We can be motivated to learn and discover new things and thereby to grow or develop ourselves. Sometimes we realize that we need new and different challenges to keep growing. We may have given a lot of ourselves towards a cause and whilst we could still give more, there is something new that gives us new and greater energy and attracts us more strongly. The older cause might then better be left to those whose fires are still burning bright for that particular challenge.

2. THE DIFFERENCE MOTIVATION CAN MAKE

Motivation can make the difference between achieving goals or not. The characteristics of the motivating force can have important implications for the sustainability of an organization as well as an individual's actions and efforts.

The right motivational formula can help you, your team or organization to:

- Create an inspiring vision for your goal.

- Take the first steps towards your goal.

- Put effort into coming up with a good plan.

- Enjoy the challenge.

- Ensure you leverage strengths.

- Help keep you focused and reduce distractions.

- Help you to endure difficult realities or obstacles and find effective ways to deal with them.

- Have the right energy to stick to a necessary course when the going gets tough.

- Deal more effectively with conflicts and make trade-offs.

In other words, it is a fuel pump that can help you and your company to keep going and growing.

3. A Model for Motivation

If we think about motivation as a force that helps keep us moving in the right direction until we reach a goal, then we can come up with a metaphor to use as a model for motivation. The right motivation will also help us, not only to persist, but also to be resourceful and to find ways around obstacles.

Let's use the metaphor of climbing a mountain. If you wish, you may think of a metaphor that is more inspiring for you and modify the words to better fit your version. This model can be adapted to best fit an individual, a group or organization.

- We need an *inspiring vision of success* – Reaching the peak and enjoying the magnificent view and sense of achievement.

- We need *a motive* – What is the blend of the four motivations that will give us the impetus to move forward and commit to our goal? What will achieving the goal give us? What will the climb itself give us aside from reaching the peak?

- We need *a plan* – A map of how to reach our goal, the peak.

- We need to believe in our plan and our ability to deliver on it. We need *realistic confidence, belief and optimism* that we can reach the peak (not dangerous or unmerited over-confidence).

- We need to give ourselves *a push* to take our first step on the route up the mountain.

- We need *a feedback loop*, of what is working well and taking us forward, and what is hindering us and how we can mitigate its negative impact.

- We need to make and communicate effective and timely *decisions*, as necessary, to stay on or adjust course.

- We need to *recognize conflict* and difficulties in the team that may hinder our successful advance and know how to deal constructively with these.

- We need a degree of *flexibility* to adjust our plan to new, changed, or learned realities.

- We need to have *subgoals* that help us reach our big goals.

- We need to *celebrate successes* with the stakeholders involved.

- We need to utilize acknowledgements of success and realistic feedback, even if it's not what we wished for, to *reinforce our confidence* and belief.

- We need to keep this *constructive approach* going in a cyclical way until we finally succeed. There may be times where we reluctantly decide to give up on our goal as we, or circumstances, have changed (i.e., We are injured or the weather becomes lethal – in this case we are more motivated to survive than to keep battling against unwinnable odds).

Such a model is useful as maintaining motivation often goes beyond our inner drivers and into the frequently harsh realities of life (see section 7 on keeping motivated). We may have strong inner motivations, but if we do not have the right mechanisms for learning, adapting and keeping up momentum, individually and as a group, we can fail to reach our goal.

When the model is applied to a group or to an organization there are, of course, the additional dimensions of motivating others and trying to achieve effective results through the team. So from a leadership point of view there are additional skills necessary, such as: selling the vision, facilitating common understandings, taking the lead, taking/committing to the first step, setting an example, walking the talk, influencing others, managing resistance to change and the political landscape etc. On an organizational level the critical skills of influencing, persuading, communicating, leading and managing are indispensable.

A well-motivated team has the advantages of being supportive and re-generative. If a normally motivated person is struggling for some reason, good management and good teams can provide the kind of support to mitigate the impact or length of time that someone is "down."

Motivation alone is never enough in an organizational setting, but without it nothing worthwhile can ever happen.

Exercise: Go through the steps of the model/metaphor in relation to yourself and facilitate it with your team. How do you rate your skills and situation on each step out of ten? What improvements should you prioritize?

Use the space below to write your notes:

_____

_____

_____

_____

_____

_____

_____

_____

_____

_____

4. A LOOK AT YOUR "A"

4.1   Your motivation to do what you do

What is your motivation for your current job? Perhaps your motivation to do it has changed over time. It may have once been fulfilling but now leaves you feeling bored or frustrated? Perhaps you desire to engage in work that is more meaningful to you?

Take a moment to think about your current motivation.

A political motivation would be because you are afraid of some external consequence of not doing that work. Perhaps it was the expectations of your family or peers that caused you to select an occupation and you remain afraid of rejection if you do not follow their expectations?

An economic motivation to do your current job might be because it seems like a good way to make money. Research shows that while monetary compensation is a necessary factor to ward off job dissatisfaction, in and of itself, money will not always create job satisfaction. If you do not find personal value or satisfaction in what you do, no salary will make the job fulfilling.

An emotional motivation to do your current job would be because you enjoy the tasks or the outcomes of what you do. The experience is pleasurable. At the end of the day, while you might be tired, you feel fulfilled and satisfied.

A deeper motivation is like a "warm fuzzy feeling" you get in your gut because you really value, enjoy and believe in what you do. When deeply motivated you simply cannot not do what you do. What you do expresses something about your deeper purpose. For example, if you are a teacher you teach because teaching fulfills you; it is not something you simply do, it is who you are. It is from this sense of awareness that "flow states" or "being in the zone" occur. The work seems effortless, energizing and creative. While potentially physically and mentally tiring, at the end of the day you may sleep with a deep sense of satisfaction knowing that you will awake refreshed and inspired to do it all over again. You love this work and you have a positive feeling not only towards yourself and the people you work with, but for your wider contribution to society too.

This is how you are able to maintain your enthusiasm over long periods of time.

4.2   Growing from negative to fulfilling motivations

Regardless of the reason, as you make changes in your life, try to ensure that your motivation is moving from "No" to "Yes!" – from something of lesser to greater value, from being driven by fear or something negative to something more fulfilling.

Negative feelings and emotions will only hold you back. A negative mind is constantly stuck in a dark place while a positive one is able to build momentum, gain enthusiasm and make progress. A positive attitude towards your life and career is essential to your success.

To reach this more positive state of mind you will need make changes and be constructive but stay true to your deep inner motivating forces.

4.3   Exploring your personal motivating forces

Write down your answers in the spaces provided:

*   Make a list in the box below of the times you have felt most committed, passionate, energized and enthusiastic:

The situations you have listed describe what "in the zone" or "in a flow state" means to you. Time passes very quickly and you are highly energized during these periods. It is good to consider all aspects and stages of your life. You may have pointed to a project, a role, a day, a special moment. What matters is that special energy.

What is it that made each item on your list special for you?

_____

_____

_____

_____

_____

Can you see common themes, links or connections between these underlying factors?

_____

_____

_____

When have you been at your most creative? This may give you some clues as to what motivates you.

_____

_____

_____

_____

_____

When have you been most confident in yourself and your decisions?

_____

_____

_____

_____

What do you consider to be your greatest accomplishments?

_____

_____

_____

_____

_____

When have you enjoyed your work the most?

_____

_____

_____

_____

_____

What talents were you using in these situations?

_____

_____

_____

_____

Which bosses have most inspired you? How did they manage to do this?

_____

_____

_____

_____

What things would you take a strong stand for?

_____

_____

_____

_____

What about the world upsets you or makes you angry?

_____

_____

_____

_____

What contribution could you make in this regard? How would it feel to make a difference in this way?

_____

_____

_____

_____

What jobs do you like to do at work when you have a choice?

_____

_____

_____

_____

What activities are you drawn to outside of work?

_____

_____

_____

_____

If money were no concern and you had all the wealth and financial security you wanted, what would you be doing?

_____

_____

_____

_____

Review your answers. Make a list of the things that you enjoy and motivate you. Keep asking the question: "What is it about X, Y and Z that most motivates me?" This will help you get to the deeper roots of your key motivating forces.

Once you have a list of things that motivate you, group them as appropriate and put them in order of importance. Try to focus on anything up to around seven factors or groupings.

You can then do a gap analysis by rating your satisfaction levels out of a maximum of 5 for each of the main aspects of your life. One way of doing this is to consider the different "roles" you play in your life – for example, as a worker, manager, friend, parent/family member, hobby enthusiast etc.

Use the space below to write any additional notes and analysis:

4.4   Career motivators assessment

On our website (www.thrive-careers.com) we have designed a free "career motivators personality test" that can help you gain a better insight into your top motivating forces and personality type. Take the test and write your results and observations below:

What were your top five "career motivators?"

_____

_____

_____

Which of the five do you feel most accurately describe you irrespective of score achieved on the assessment?

_____

_____

_____

Are your top five adequately catered for in your role and in your organization?

_____

_____

_____

Sometimes we aren't doing enough of what motivates us. Could you possibly do more of something or make changes at work to address an ignored "career motivator?"

_____

_____

_____

_____

If you are very motivated by meaning and service, for example, many corporations have charity and community service projects you could be involved in. If these kinds of projects are not in place maybe you can contact human resources or your boss about how the business can contribute to the community and the environment in a way that's positive for the business too?

Another example would be if you are very results oriented and your boss and teammates haven't developed much of a habit of celebrating small and big achievements. You can start by celebrating the achievements of those around you. Where possible, build anticipation and promote a genuine effort amongst the team towards achieving targets. When you motivate and praise others they often return the favor.

Does your organization encourage anything that demotivates you? If so, are these detrimental to your motivation or are you able to not let them impact you? For instance, organizations heavily centered on meaning and service can sometimes be off-putting to material individuals and vice versa.

_____

_____

_____

_____

_____

4.5   Motivation blockers

There are always things that demotivate us, make us feel sad or "down." If you also look to understand these you can attempt to stop bad habits and steer away from potential hazards to your motivation.

List in the box below the times that you have felt most lethargic and lacking in energy, not just physically tired, but really demotivated.

What about each situation sucked out your energy and demotivated you? Look for a deeper understanding of the root causes.

_____

_____

_____

_____

_____

_____

What bores you?

_____

_____

_____

_____

What type of people or what behaviors sap your enthusiasm?

_____

_____

_____

_____

What types of bosses or what leadership behaviors demotivate you? What is it about these bosses/leaders that has this effect on you?

_____

_____

_____

_____

5. A Look at the "A" of your Team & Organization

To motivate others you must first be motivated yourself. People can easily sense if you are genuinely motivated or not. You may have a technically brilliant strategy and plan, but if you are not passionate about it others will inherently sense it. So it's right that you look at yourself first in section 4 before moving on to motivating others.

5.1   Motivating people as individuals

Becoming a proficient motivator depends on many factors. If you look at your own answers to the questions in section 4 you can see how individual your own motivating forces and motivation blockers can be. In a team of several people this complexity increases. You may be doing various things correctly to motivate people, but sometimes seemingly small or irrational things can be important blockers for other people.

According to a famous study by Rewick and Lawler (1978), the top motivating forces at work are: 1. Job challenge, 2. Accomplishing something worthwhile, 3. Learning new things, 4. Personal development, and 5. Autonomy. These were arrived at statistically therefore we should be careful to not follow data blindly and generalize.

Symptoms of poor motivation can include issues with productivity, quality, absenteeism and poor punctuality, resignations, complaints, negative forms of conflict and bad cross-functional relations. What are the indicators like in your organization or team? How well do they benchmark against competitors or other departments?

Are you using a staff satisfaction survey? Is it professionally managed in a way that gives staff anonymity? Are you acting on the necessary points of action and interacting with staff in a way that comes up with constructive plausible solutions to improve engagement and motivation?

What do you think would be the answers to section 4 for each of your staff or direct reports?

Many managers and leaders assume they know what motivates their staff. It is a good practice to learn to ask the sorts of questions mentioned here using a technique called "Appreciative Inquiry" and to actively listen to the answers. For example, try asking someone when they felt most energized at work. Listen to their answer and ask them to explain more about what made it so motivating. Ask them for more examples from other moments in time. Most people love telling these stories about themselves and they really reveal a lot about the person. So listen carefully!

5.2   Rewards

To keep your employees motivated, or improve their motivation if it has been lacking, you need to know how to reward them when they do good work. To do this well you need to understand what they expect to get out of their job and what keeps them happy to be doing their job. A good exercise is to think of one of your employees and check off the three rewards you think the person most needs from their work.

*Rewards checklist**

☐   Good pay

☐   Good promotion prospects

☐   Official perks and benefits

☐   Unofficial perks and benefits

☐   As much free time as possible

☐   Satisfaction of working on highly important projects

☐   Gaining new expertise

☐   Easy and undemanding routine work

☐   Changing and variable work

☐   Contributing to new business endeavours

☐   Status and power

☐   Good working conditions

☐   Plenty of guidance and support

☐   Freedom to decide how to work

☐   Having good relationships with clients/customers

☐   Having good relationships with work colleagues

☐   Being respected in the workplace

☐   Being respected by people outside the company

☐   Reduced office hours or work structured around lifestyle

☐   Contributing to society and social projects

*A printable copy of this checklist is available on Thrive's website.

Maybe there are other rewards you can think of that are appropriate for this employee?

_____

_____

_____

_____

How about your other reports or employees? Which rewards would they most expect to receive?

_____

_____

_____

_____

_____

Do your reports or employees vary in the kinds of rewards they want to receive?

Yes ☐ No ☐

Is there any way you could find out more about the kinds of rewards your employees enjoy now, would like to have or expect to have?

_____

_____

_____

_____

Can you think of changes you can make to allow for new rewards that employees aren't expecting to receive?

_____

_____

_____

_____

5.3   How to be better at rewarding employees

Remuneration and rewards can be complex areas and large companies often have specialists focused on these. The complexities can include legislation, market practices and comparisons, technical measures of job sizes and grades, in-company relativities and cultural preferences for individual versus team-based performance rewards. There is also the aspect of fixed and variable costs – fixed salary and variable performance based remuneration – and deciding what suits the activity and development stage of the organization better.

Are most of the rewards presently available for your employees attainable simply by keeping their job? If this is the case, is there any way you can create or modify rewards so that a higher proportion of overall remuneration and benefits is obtainable when employees are performing well? Are any of these possible rewards ones that your employees would value and can be linked to performance? This isn't about suddenly stripping employees of chunks of their salaries and making their pay heavily performance-related – that would cause a lot of unease. In some countries it's illegal. Quite possibly your organization pays employees 95-100% of their total remuneration pay in the form of a salary. Could you maybe look at increasing performance-related pay or prizes for success and excellence? In addition to these, non-material rewards are important too. Taking your time to praise an employee in front of their colleagues is often an important part of overall recognition. Such recognition is unlikely to fully compensate for low or unfair levels of remuneration, but other things being equal, can make a big difference in retaining and encouraging good staff.

Also important is how you express to staff what they have to do to obtain rewards. A reward here can also be a promotion, a new career or project opportunity. You can provide an insight into this through their job description or a written set of objectives and descriptions of standards. Also, when praising or criticizing you have to be clear what it is you liked and disliked and how this compares with the standards you expect. Give them encouragement; show that you believe they are capable of achieving these standards if they have failed to do so. Your feedback should be prompt and supportive, whether praising or giving constructive criticism.

As a boss you also have to keep your word with regards to rewards for performance. If you have promised a reward and the employee succeeds they naturally expect to receive this award. Failure to do so will damage their motivation and the trust and respect they had for you as a boss. In some cases it will give employees a reason to leave the company. Thus, it is important that as far as possible rewards are given in a transparent and fairly objective manner, rather than being highly subjective.

Summing up: You want to give relevant rewards to staff, make sure the rewards incentivize excellent, not average work, and keep your promise on delivering rewards for progress and performance.

5.4 Motivating your team or organization as a whole

- How skilled are you at motivating others?

- Do you know how others rate you in this aspect of your leadership and management?

- If you're unsure then how can you get the feedback and support you need to get to the next level?

Skilled motivators exercise

Rate yourself on each of these factors out of a maximum score of five. You can ask some or all of your reports to rate you on each item for further insight into your abilities as a motivator.

☐ Creates an environment and atmosphere in which people want to do their best.

☐ Creates an environment where people can challenge and bring difficult issues to the table.

☐ Creates an environment where mistakes are treated appropriately. An environment where people can learn from mistakes and be supported and coached to become more skilled and innovative.

☐ Can motivate a wide variety of personalities and contributors, employing different tailored approaches to each individual.

☐ Makes sure the team understands its objectives, are committed to the task and clearly understand the contribution of each member of the team to the overall objective.

☐ Knows how to build mutual trust with employees.

☐ Knows the keys to each individual's attention and drive and how to leverage them positively and fairly.

☐ Knows how to integrate their messages, actions and decisions to appeal as far as possible to both individual and team motivations.

☐ Helps people feel they belong to the team. Is an inclusive and friendly team-builder.

☐ Wants projects to succeed not just for them as individuals but for the whole team.

☐ Delegates decisions and tasks effectively and fairly – allowing team members to gain competence, experience and stretch their skills.

☐ Gets timely and quality input from others and shares accountability and recognition.

☐ Helps each individual understand the value and importance of their contribution.

☐ Is someone who others recognize as consistently capable of bringing out their best.

☐ Knows when it's necessary to be tough – with whom and in the right format (often in a one-to-one meeting).

☐ Good communicator of the expectations for performance and how under-performance will be transformed or dealt with as necessary.

☐ Reads others well – picks up verbal and non-verbal cues.

☐ Uses open questions and truly listens to answers. Holds back judgement and does not stereotype people.

☐ Understands the impact they have on others, both positive and negative, obvious and subtle, and seeks feedback on their behaviors in a way that will lead to honest and useful answers.

6. GETTING TO YOUR "B"

Your assessment of where you are, what is going well and what can be improved helps you to define and have a clear vision of where it is you are trying to get to. We call this getting from where you "Are" to where you want to "Be."

In general terms we need to understand what we need to:

- Start doing, which we are not doing.
- Stop doing, which is holding us back.
- Keep doing that which we are doing well and makes a difference.
- Do more of that which we don't do enough of.
- Do less of that which we still need to do but should do less often.

To get to **B** we will need to have challenges – new opportunities to learn, to practice and grow. We also will need the resources, learning, guidance and on-going feedback and encouragement of others.

Fill in the spaces with your thoughts on what you should and shouldn't be doing to keep yourself motivated. If you can't come up with much yet, then don't worry. Return to this section once you have read through the tips to follow!

Start doing –

_____

_____

_____

_____

Stop doing –

_____

_____

_____

_____

Keep doing –

_____

_____

_____

_____

Do more of –

_____

_____

_____

_____

Do less of –

_____

_____

_____

_____

7. TIPS TO KEEP YOURSELF MOTIVATED

- *Have a vision* – It cannot be stressed enough how important the power of the mind is. Our minds are capable of giving us strength or making us feel vulnerable, helping us imagine the impossible and then make it possible, and to transport ourselves into situations that haven't yet happened or we have never experienced before. Create a vivid picture in your mind of where you want your career to be heading. Think about what you are doing, what you are achieving, what is happening around you and how this all feels. If you ever feel demotivated close your eyes for a few seconds and visualize this image you are striving towards. It's a simple method of keeping yourself in line with your objectives and giving you the motivation to get there.

- *Have goals* – Now that you have a vision, set yourself written goals to help you get there. Small daily goals, weekly, monthly and yearly goals are all equally important to keep yourself motivated. Achieving small goals will propel you to ultimately achieve the big goals you have set for yourself, so don't forget to aim for small wins that get you to the finish line! Without setting big goals for yourself it can be difficult to be motivated to achieve the small ones. For example, if someone wants to lose weight, simply aiming to drop by 2 pounds by next week isn't going to be good enough. You want to aim to be 80 pounds thinner and look great while setting smaller goals until you get there. This may be really simple and obvious but combining goals with the other tips can be very powerful.

- *Reward yourself for achievements* – So you've finished your report for the day, now treat yourself to a few drinks with friends. You reached your sales target for the month – go play a game of tennis. Your team won over a new client – buy that gadget you've had your eyes on for months. Whatever motivates you, treat yourself for achieving your goals. Setting goals and achieving them is certainly fun, motivating and encouraging but an additional treat can be a great motivator too. This motivation technique does require commitment. If you keep treating yourself to episodes of your favorite TV show when you haven't done the work you are doing yourself a big disservice. Treats are for achievements and achievements only. For the sake of your finances you might want to make sure not all your rewards are material in nature! Reward yourself with what gives you pleasure.

- *Keep a healthy work/life balance* – If you are overworking yourself you will be tired, stressed and feeling the blues. Your body can react to stress and tiredness with bouts of depression, insomnia, irritability and insomnia (American Institute of Stress). All of these effects of stress on the brain will not be good for your mental state or motivation and can in fact form a very serious vicious cycle. For our bodies and minds to be at their most productive and motivated we need our sleep, our leisure time and to maintain a healthy lifestyle. Good quality sleep is important for optimal brain functionality and being in a good mood to work. Experts say most people need about 7-8 hours a day for optimal performance. Leisure time, even if only for half an hour, allows us to relax, stimulate our minds in new ways and is often a time we can use for reflection. A healthy diet and lifestyle do have positive effects on our performance and mood. A diet composed of too many fatty foods with few vitamins and varied nutrients unbalance the chemicals in our body and consequently affect our mood. Similarly, snacking on too many high sugar foods and drinks can take our mood on a roller coaster ride of highs and lows, not exactly the way to keep motivated throughout the 8 hours in the office is it? Many people find exercise is a good way to unwind and balance the body's chemicals.

- *Remind yourself why you are working* – What are the things that keep you working at the job you do? Feeding and paying for your children's school? Expressing your creativity? Making a difference? Seeing the business grow?

  On a separate piece of paper, or maybe a page of your agenda, write down the things that keep you going to work. If you need a bit of motivation, look back at this and keep going. If you truly have no reason to work in your current job and can't find meaning in what you do, it may be that you need a career change.

- *Transforming negative thinking into positive questions* – Our subconscious minds can often play tricks on us, reducing our choices and keeping us sometimes from the success we are looking for.

  Individually we need to become aware of the "little voice" in our head that can surface when we feel insecure or over-confident. It is remarkable how this voice can limit our self-belief or ability to act effectively. This is our subconscious mind in action.

Repeating a challenging or positive mantra – an affirmation of some kind – can help us in times of challenge, however, sometimes we don't really "buy" them. For example, an athlete can keep telling himself over and over that he can achieve some target, that he can "do it." But sometimes during this repetition another "little voice" from somewhere (the subconscious) rises and sheds doubt on, or questions, the positive affirmation.

There is evidence that much of the brain is formed to answer questions and solve problems. Questions can go around and around in our minds. We know that we can fall asleep with a problem or question in our mind and the solution or answer can pop out when we awaken. This emphasizes the power of questions and the subconscious mind's ability to seek for and find answers.

So it is often the case that our minds get "stuck" on negative questions for which our minds can find no satisfactory answer. They just keep surfacing the same old doubts and fears.

If we couple the idea of an affirmation with the power of questions we can come up with a powerful and affirming question to repeat to ourselves. First, we need to find or realize what is the core underlying negative or doubting question going around in our mind. Then we can then apply some positive psychology and transform it into a positive question that the subconscious will then work on seeking positive self-affirming answers.

For example, John finds himself at a moment that he knows he could lighten-up and be humorous, but he catches his "little voice" saying to himself: "What's the point? Surely if I remain serious they will respect me more and just get on with the job?" Here a positive question that he can repeat regularly to himself could be: "Why am I getting better and better at lightening up so people can relax and laugh with me whilst maintaining their respect and loyalty towards me?"

It helps to say these positive enabling questions to ourselves before we sleep and on awakening. Our subconscious minds can then seek the transformational answers that we have lacked. Repetition can help diminish and override the negative question that has impacted us. We can also use it at the time the old voice starts raising its negativity.

The feeling of being stuck is a very real motivation buster. This technique can help us use the power of our subconscious mind to find solutions to our issues and, in doing so, motivate us even further.

- *Try upbeat music* – Music has the ability to change our mood so why not try listening to a collection of upbeat music. Separate the tracks that make you feel happy and make you want to get things done. Think about what kind of music you might put on if you had a lot of cleaning or DIY to do in your house! Consider filing your music digitally by the mood it induces for you. For example, high speed or high energy, reflective, inspirational, creative energy etc. Then you can easily tap into the music you need depending on the task at hand.

- *Make your work fun* – A few things at work can seem a little boring to us. Perhaps bigger tasks are starting to daunt us too. Our mind-set is crucial to whether we feel we want to complete a task or not. Stop for a second and think about ways to make your work more fun. Is it making a few jokes with your colleagues while you do the accounts? Could doing a little dance or singing a silly song do the trick? Maybe the way you perform a task needs to be more fun? Thought about treating yourself to a chocolate for every paragraph you write? Remember the tip on rewards – they work wonders!

- *Acknowledge possible setbacks* – Even if you are currently motivated it can be good to accept there could be setbacks along the way. These may be times when things become more difficult due to external reasons or you see a dip in your motivation. If you acknowledge these setbacks are inevitable but won't stop you from achieving your goal, you will press on when the going gets tough.

- *Share objectives publicly* – This might not be a good idea for everyone or every goal. If you are seeking to be promoted you might want to keep that to yourself and not tell everyone about it. But say you have a smaller personal goal that would be OK to share. By sharing with others, certain personality types will want to achieve this goal to avoid personal embarrassment.

- *Motivational friendships* – Those we have around us can have a strong effect on our lives. Friends that are very negative, love whining and criticizing will drag you down. Think about keeping your distance from very negative people when you need to motivate yourself. In fact those friendships that are supportive, positive and lively are just what you DO need to keep motivated.

- *Frame it!* – Keep special things that inspire you close to hand. For example, frame special quotes or pictures that inspire and motivate you. Make sure these visual cues really bring out positive emotions within you as emotional and deep motivations are often the strongest and most enduring ones. When you need a boost you'll have that reminder close by to stop you from procrastinating or feeling depressed.

8. TIPS TO KEEP YOUR TEAM MOTIVATED

- *Watch the way you treat others* – Treat your team with the respect, support, interest and consideration you expect others to have towards you. People are motivated to work for bosses who they like and respect. A leader can start earning this by being a good listener, being challenging yet helpful, saying a simple "thank you," acknowledging and celebrating successes and achievements made by your staff. The *A to B Guide to Delegation* offers good advice on what it takes to get teams to complete tasks successfully. By making sure you are doing the basics you can move on to motivating your team in other ways. Managers who ignore this tip are missing the easiest, yet one of the most meaningful, ways of motivating a team.

- *Think beyond the obvious job motivations* – Ask most managers how to motivate their team and they will commonly answer "give them a raise, praise and inspire, offer a promotion." Yes these do motivate people but only superficially and for a short period of time. The joy of the promotion could last a few months if it's what the employee wanted, the happiness from a pay rise only lasts a few weeks, and that of a few nice comments only for a day or maybe a few hours. To motivate continually you have to find people's intrinsic motivating forces. Research has shown employees are intrinsically motivated by a challenging job, accomplishing something they find meaningful, learning something new, developing as a person, and autonomy.

- *Intelligent goal setting* – Don't just set goals for your employees and dish them out. Think about these goals. Are they reasonable and achievable? Are they helping stretch employees at the same time? Discuss the goals with your team and let them participate in the goal-making process as appropriate. They will want to achieve things they are motivated by and believe are feasible but not too easy. Allowing them to participate will help you get a sense of all these measures: Feasible? How easy/hard? What aspects motivate them within each goal?

- *Don't be judgemental* – Just because you are motivated by money and status doesn't allow you to look negatively at those who are motivated by personal growth and creativity, and vice versa. Whatever it is that people value, believe in and are motivated by, you should be open-minded and respectful of. You will be incapable of motivating people who you view as inferior, crazy or weird.

- *Be open and get to know your employees* – Openness is key to getting to know people better. If you give people something, they tend to return the favor. Starting a conversation about your weekend, your holiday or your kids will likely get employees talking back about things that are personal to them. You want employees to respect you but also feel they can talk to you. A stronger relationship will help you understand your employees better and motivate them on a personal level. A good test of an employee relationship is to write a list of a few things about your staff member's life outside work. We aren't talking about gossip here. What are their hobbies? What music, books and films do they like? What would they do on a Friday night? What things are important to them outside the workplace – religion, family, dancing, cooking, gardening, sports, travel?

- *Bring meaning to the workplace* – Let employees plan and participate in project development. Give them the authority and autonomy to work well on these projects. Is the project intrinsically motivating for the parties involved? Some smaller tasks are not vastly motivating but as long as you help employees see it as part of something bigger and important it will be meaningful to them. Ask your employees for their opinions on important issues.

- *Give and seek constructive feedback* – If you have sought an understanding of what motivates an employee and have developed good rapport and trust between you, then you will be in a good position to energize and develop them.

It's important to have good ongoing dialogue in which you and the other person seek and give each other feedback on what's working well, what's appreciated and what could go better. It is also vital for managers to be clear and fair in how they deal with lack of employee performance. Listen first to their story as to why and how things haven't been working well before expressing your views. Think about being encouraging by giving two or three genuine positives to each suggestion for improvement. You want to encourage employees to perform better, not to demoralize them. Share your employee's vision of their own development and celebrate their successes along the way.

- *Combine regular informal feedback with periodic formal performance appraisals and developmental reviews* – Ideally, the previous point is well aligned with the formal half-year or annual performance appraisal processes that many organizations have as part of their normal personnel procedures. Good motivators don't wait for the formal review to praise or give constructive feedback to an employee. They integrate their approach – the longer-term thinking of the formal procedures with feedback on daily activities.

- *Learn to use your coaching skills* – Often when someone has a challenge or difficulty they can find the right solution or answer for themselves aided by your coaching. This entails using good questions to help someone diagnose a situation, review the options and potential outcomes themselves, helping them towards their own action plan. This kind of skilled facilitation can create a deeper and more lasting learning experience for someone than merely telling them what to do. It can also lead to someone being more motivated to go ahead on their own terms than on someone else's.

- *Make the workplace a fun place to be* – Much like motivating ourselves we can motivate others by making work fun. If the accounting office has a bored group of staff crunching the monthly figures why not throw in a bit of music or start a competition?

- *Create synergy in the team* – Most people love working in a team where there is trust and people know and leverage each others' strengths, contributions and potential. Their work achieves the wonder of synergy where "one plus one equals three," or in other words, something special happens in the way different personalities with different skills create something more astounding than the individuals ever could by working alone.

It is possible though that some people, even after good support and coaching, can still act as dampeners to this type of group synergy. Maybe their values or the way they like to behave and operate just don't go well with the team and it would be better for the individual and the team if he or she went somewhere they were better suited. This means selecting the right people, not just with the right skills, but also the right values and behaviors for the team in the first place. Learn how to cross-check for these aspects in when interviewing potential additions to your team.

In short, people are motivated by someone who cares for them and trusts them. They are motivated by those who respect their professionalism and expertise as well as someone who combines challenges and support in the right way.

9. YOUR A TO B ACTION PLAN

Step 1

Review your answers and notes from the guidebook. This will include tips and ideas that you marked as resonating. Consolidate these or highlight the most important aspects in a specific color.

On the Challenge-Priority Brainstorming Chart (see Appendix) list challenges you have picked up from this guidebook, however small they may be.

Stand back from your list and see what links and connections there are – maybe use a different color to highlight challenges that have a similar source such as fear of failing, communication difficulties, procrastination etc.

If possible, group these items under headings or concepts that you think appropriate – use your intuition and creativity here. Go as much with your feelings as your logical mind.

If you have several items for potential action, number them in priority order. There tends to be something we need to address first because it is more important to us or will give us the most benefits.

Take your top priority challenge and move on to your Thrive Action Plan (see Appendix).

Step 2

Take this top grouping/item you identified in your Challenge-Priority Brainstorming Chart.

What is the right goal or **B** here? What is going to make the most significant difference?

Try writing the goal down on a separate sheet of paper in three different ways. Which one do you find most compelling? What is it that makes it so? Think about why achieving this goal will help and what you will gain from it.

Studies have shown that people who can create a vivid image of what their achievement will look and feel like are more likely to achieve it. Take your time to really immerse yourself in this image. What you feel when you think of this image should be used as a tool to motivate yourself along your journey.

Step 3

Build on the goal to make it SMART:

Specific: As detailed and real as possible – something you can visualize clearly if you are a visual person.

Measurable: Make sure you have quantitative targets for the activity itself and the impact or outcomes you want too.

Attainable: You sense it's a stretch but you know you can do it!

Realistic: Think of the practical aspects that are necessary for success – the resources, support, strategies and tactics that will bring you success. You should be able to list these on the Thrive Action Plan, if you struggle, then your goal is possibly not realistic enough.

Timed: Build in specific deadlines – for the big steps and completion. These can be further broken down into daily or weekly goals if, for example, you need to grow your comfort zone bit by bit, day by day. Think stepping stones!

Example of a SMART motivation improvement goal:

"I will become a highly motivated person who will not fall victim to procrastination and this will be noticed by my colleagues and managers. I will dedicate 2 hours a day to routine tasks, one hour in the morning and one in the afternoon. In between these I will focus on pleasing my customers, as this makes me feel good, and aim to beat my profit targets to achieve the bonus I want for a new motorcycle.

Should I feel tired or demotivated I shall take a timed 5 minute break to either exercise, have a coffee or relax before resuming my workload. I will remind myself of my passion for customer service and making money during the day through a motivation pocket book I'll write and draw in starting next week.

I will measure my daily sales against targets and also my efficient use of time. At the end of each week I'll evaluate how focused and successful I have been throughout the week. If I have avoided procrastinating, I'll treat myself to a new CD and eventually a new motorcycle if all goes well!"

Step 4

Get going on your first action. This should be within a week from now.

Step 5

You need to get the support resources lined up.

It helps if you can inform a few well-selected individuals from your friends or family to share the goal with, seek their feedback and suggestions of how you can do things better to achieve your goal. As you move forward they can give you further valuable feedback on your progress as well as encouragement.

Think about who encourages you best, who gives you the best advice, who helps you when you are in difficulty and who may have the same developmental challenge and can go on the journey with you. Avoid sharing your goal with negative or cynical people who are likely only to discourage you.

Decide on who are the best people to help you: usually a group of 1-3 mentors.

Step 6

As investigated in section 4 of this guidebook there will be barriers and motivation blockers to your success in motivating yourself and others.

What were the main motivation blockers you highlighted? Think also about how you plan to overcome these inevitable barriers and how you can use your support system to push you past these!

Step 7

Decide on the frequency you are going to review your progress towards your goal – often weekly works well. What has worked well and what lessons have been learned?

Build on the successes and lessons learned and plan your next week's activities.

If you get discouraged or have a setback, don't be too hard on yourself. This can happen. After doing something that leaves you feeling positive and relaxed build on the positive momentum to press forward with your goals. Look for inspiration in this guidebook.

Be determined to take some positives out of the setback.

Ask if your goal or your sub-steps are too stretched and you need to re-calibrate or take longer. Sometimes behavioral change programs can take nine months or so!

If you really get stuck, seek help from a good mentor or coach.

Keep going.

Step 8

Success! Well done.

10. KEY POINT SUMMARY

Throughout this guidebook you will have attempted to uncover the root causes of both personal and organizational motivation problems by asking probing questions and pushing to seek feedback from those around you. By analyzing the roots of your motivational issues you can hopefully make steps towards overcoming these. Use the techniques and tips highlighted to your full advantage, taking what you feel is of most use and possibly discarding ideas you feel aren't too relevant to your specific case. Whether your greatest struggle has been motivating yourself or motivating others, the secret to better motivation lies within our own minds. We have to ultimately uncover our inner callings and equipped with this information use it to give us the energy and desire to move forward with our careers and lives.

11. USEFUL EXTRA READING

Readers of this guidebook will often find some of Thrive's other books of especially good use.

If you or your employees struggle with procrastination and forming a cohesive plan to perform tasks you will enjoy reading the *A to B Guide to Prioritization*. This guidebook will help you with various methods of organizing your mind to achieve what you need to in the workplace.

If you are motivated by creative challenges and thinking outside the box the *A to B Guide to Creativity* will be an interesting read. It contains a large list of tips on building your creative skills and pushing your mind to think in new directions.

Your boss might be a huge source of demotivation for you. If this is the case you won't regret reading the *A to B Guide to Dealing with Difficult Bosses* as it explores methods to tackle various boss personality types and build a better relationship with your boss. Combined with this guidebook you can hopefully find the secrets to bring back the fun you used to have at work.

References and recommendations:

Amabile, Teresa M. and Steven J. Kramer. "Inner Work Life: Understanding the Subtext of Business Performance" Harvard Business Review. 01 May 2007. Web. 15 Feb. 2012. <http://www.hbr.org/2007/05/inner-work-life-understanding-the-subtext-of-business-performance/ar/1>

Amabile, Teresa M. and Steven J. Kramer. "How leaders kill meaning at work" McKinsey Quarterly. Jan 2012. Web. 15 Feb. 2012. <http://www.mckinseyquarterly.com/How_leaders_kill_meaning_at_work_2910>

American Institute of Stress. 2012. The American Institute of Stress. 15 Feb. 2012 <http://www.stress.org/>.

Buckingham, Marcus. "What Great Managers Do" Harvard Business Review. 01 Mar. 2005. Web. 15 Feb. 2012. <http://www.hbr.org/2005/03/what-great-managers-do/ar/1>

Herzberg, Frederick. "One More Time: How Do You Motivate Employees?" 01 Jan. 2003. Web. 15 Feb 2012. <http://www.hbr.org/2003/01/one-more-time-how-do-you-motivate-employees/ar/1>

Percy, Ian. *Going Deep: Exploring Spirituality in Life and Leadership.* Toronto: Macmillan Canada, 1997. Print.

Renwick, P. A. and Lawler, E. E. (1978). What you really want from your job. *Psychology Today*, May, 53-65.

Thomas, Kenneth W. *Intrinsic Motivation at Work: Building Energy & Commitment.* San Francisco: Berrett-Koehler Publishers, Inc. 2000. Print.

12. OTHER USEFUL THRIVE RESOURCES

This guidebook is designed to give you as much support and challenge as possible. Perhaps you would also appreciate a more in-depth course in which you have access to an experienced mentor to help keep you on track with your personal learning and to support you on your areas of greatest personal difficulty. The Motivation Mentor Course found on the Thrive website does just that. Additionally, if you have isolated specific areas that you are struggling to achieve, you may appreciate direct access to a mentor also through the "Mentor Courses" section of the website (www.thrive-careers.com).

ABOUT THE AUTHOR

Brian Guest is a former CEO with an extensive international career in Fortune 100 companies. Based on his experience working at various management levels and motivated by a desire to help others achieve their potential he decided to begin a career as an international executive coach.

He obtained an M.A. in Natural Sciences from the University of Cambridge, England, in 1978. Brian is also qualified as an ACA (Chartered Accountant, the UK equivalent of a CPA) in 1981.

In 1982 he began his international career on joining the American International Group (then a Fortune 100 company, the largest global insurer) as an international auditor. He was promoted to audit management and worked in the USA, Latin America, Caribbean, Europe and Africa.

In 1987 he joined Royal Insurance (now RSA) and worked in financial management in the international division.

Joining Commercial Union (now Aviva plc, 2011 Fortune Global 500 number 64) three years later, he worked in business development, holding various positions including being the General Manager for Hong Kong and Regional Director for Latin America.

In 1997 he began working in the HSBC Group (2011 Fortune Global 500 number 46) and his responsibilities over an eight year period included being CEO for the US$500mn Brazilian insurance business with 1,500 staff as well as Chief Underwriting Officer for Latin America. During this time his division received two national prizes for best performing insurer.

APPENDIX

CHALLENGE-PRIORITY BRAINSTORMING CHART

What are my challenges/problem areas?

Why are they challenges? What specific problems need to be addressed?

Can I divide my challenges/problem areas into categories?

Challenge	Priority

Thrive Action Plan

1. Challenge	What challenge am I addressing?
2. Goals	Based on my challenge, what goal can I set myself? Do I have a motivating image of the final result? Yes/No
3. SMART Goals	Use the SMART goals system to build on your goal. Specific details: How will I measure it? Time frames & deadlines: Is my goal attainable and realistic? Yes/No
4. First Step	My first step towards achieving this goal is... By when?
5. Support System	Who will be my mentors/support? What skills and resources do I have? Do I need any additional training?
6. Barriers	Possible barriers that could get in my way:
7. Review	Frequency of progress reviews & contingency plan:

ADDITIONAL NOTES

www.ingramcontent.com/pod-product-compliance
Lightning Source LLC
Chambersburg PA
CBHW070819210326
41520CB00011B/2016